10 Free Strategies

for

Internet Marketing

By Jay Berkowitz

Author Disclosure: Some of the people quoted or mentioned in this e-book are my friends and I have business relationships with several of the companies mentioned or profiled.

About the Author

Jay Berkowitz is the CEO of **www.TenGoldenRules.com**, an internet marketing agency based in Boca Raton, Florida. Jay has more than 20 years of traditional and Internet marketing experience and he has worked with Fortune 500 brands such as McDonald's, Coca-Cola, AT&T and Sprint. Today, his focus is helping small businesses and individuals learn about Internet marketing and achieve their Internet marketing goals.

Working with the University of San Francisco, Jay also developed The Internet Marketing Masters Certificate course curriculum. He is also active in numerous marketing associations: he is the founder of **www.InternetMarketingClub.org**; Past President of the American Marketing Association South Florida Chapter; a Founding Board Member of the South Florida Interactive

Marketing Association; and he serves as Co-Chairman of the Research Committee for SEMPO, the Search Engine Marketing Professionals Organization.

> *"Jay offers a rare combination of insightful, cutting-edge perspective on the Web world and tested, hit-the-ground-running online marketing tactics. I recommend Ten Golden Rules to anyone who wants to maximize their Internet potential, online demand generation, or e-commerce opportunity."*

> —Karen Talavera, President, Synchronicity

Table of Contents

#1:

Maximize Web Site Traffic by Using Free Search Engine Optimization SEO Techniques

Free SEO techniques? It sounds too good to be true, right? Believe it or not, there are plenty of ways to optimize your Web site without paying a dime to anyone. With some time and effort, you can boost traffic to your Web site without breaking the bank.

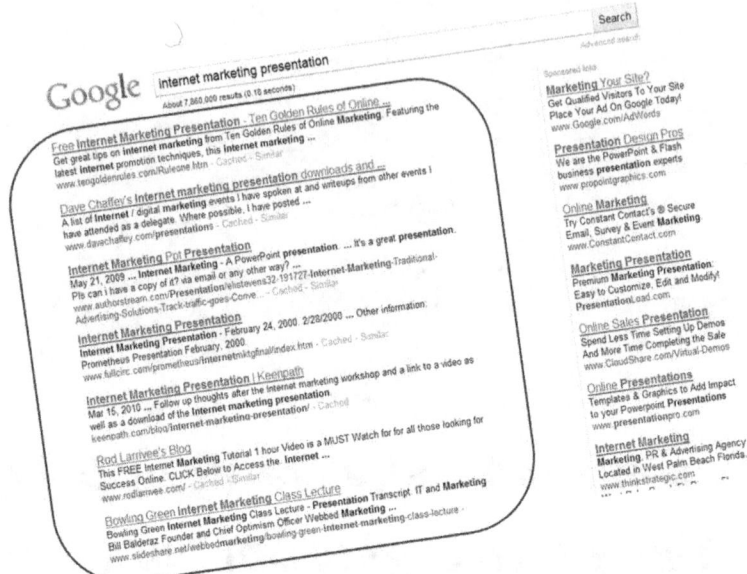

Free, or "natural" search results, show up on the left side of a search.

Search engines offer both paid and free results. For most search engines, paid results are shown at the top of the page and in a column to the right of the page. The free – or natural results – show up on the left side of a search.

Each month, people conduct over one billion searches and over 70% of those are on Google-owned properties. They are looking for your product and services – here's how to get found…

Find the Right Words

The most important part of your Web site for Google is 'copy' – the words on your pages. Other content, such as pictures and Flash designs, may make your site more visually appealing, but they do very little to help search engines find your pages.

Each page of your Web site should ideally have **250 to 1000 words of copy**. And not just any copy, but copy that contains relevant keywords, i.e., **the words that people use to search for your products or services.**

Target two or three keyword phrases per page and repeat each of them two to three times on the page. If your site has 50 pages and you have three target phrases on every page, you're giving yourself the opportunity to rank for 150 keyword phrases.

Where do you find the *RIGHT* words? Keyword Research Tools are the answer:

Google's FREE Keyword Tool

https://adwords.google.com/keywordtool

You can enter your own keyword phrases to find additional ones, or enter an existing Website URL to find keywords related to the content on the page.

Google's free keyword tool lets you find additional keyword phrases after entering your own keyword or an existing Website URL

Two other tools are www.Wordtracker.com and www.KeywordDiscovery.com. Each offers a free trial, but you'll have to subscribe for the full product.

Not only do these tools suggest keyword phrases for you, but they also show you how frequently people are searching for each phrase. The trick is to look for keyword phrases that are highly searched, but not seeing high competition.

Build Links *TO* Your Web Site

You can also help the search engines discover your Web site and boost your traffic by building links to your site, which are *active links on other Websites that link directly to your Website*. Search engines consider links to your site as a "vote" for your Website, because a vote from another site indicates that your site is important.

And it's not just the quantity of links that matter, but the quality or relevance of the sites linking to you, meaning "is there a valid relationship between the two sites?" Search engines use highly sophisticated formulae to rank Web pages and determine relevancy. You could have 5,000 links to your Web site, but if they come from sites that have nothing remotely in common with yours, they will likely have little impact on your site ranking.

This is a backlink to my Website from a listing about me on the Search Engine Marketing Professionals Organization Website, which is directly related to what my site is all about.

That's great to know. Now – how do I build links to my site?

One way to build links to your site is to get listed in Web directories, such as:

- DMOZ Open Directory Project: www.dmoz.org and
- Yahoo!: https://siteexplorer.search.yahoo.com/submit

While you likely won't get much traffic directly from a DMOZ or Yahoo! directory listing, having a link from them *will* boost your credibility in Google, Yahoo!, and MSN/Bing search results. This helps make your Website more important in the eyes of the search engines. If the search engines see you are linked from DMOZ or Yahoo!'s directory, it will improve your site's authority and rank you higher.

Where else can you get links TO your Website?

Take advantage of every opportunity you have to build relevant links to your Website.

- Are you a member of an industry association? Get them to link to your site.
- Do you have vendor relationships? Ask them to link from their site to yours.
- Everyone is looking for content on their sites – guest articles and guest blog posts are great ways to get industry-relevant and valuable links to your site

By all means, leave no stone unturned when it comes to building relevant links to your site.

Step 3: Create Website Meta Tags

The final piece of the search engine puzzle is to add meta tags to every page of your Website. Meta tags are descriptors that appear at the beginning of the HTML code for each page. They don't appear on the page, but search engines see them and incorporate them as part of their ranking algorithms.

There are several main types of meta tags: title, description, and keywords. Additionally, header tags – like H1 and H2 – alt tags, and image descriptions will all be read by the search engines. Within the HTML code, meta tags look like this:

```
<title>Title of Your Site</title>
<meta name="description" content="Description
of your site here">
<meta name="keywords" content="keywords
separated by commas">
```

The title tag is the most important. In search results, whatever is inside the <title> </title> tags shows up as the link to your site. You know the description of your site that shows up in a search page on Google? That's often from the meta description tag, so it's important to write highly targeted titles and descriptions for search engine ranking.

You should also include meta tags for every page of your site. The title and description should be different for each page, and the meta keywords should be included in the copy on that page.

The title tag should include up to 12 words, including the most important one or two keyword phrases that you used in the SEO Web page copy appearing on that page itself, with either the company name or Website at the end of the title. Here's the title tag on www.TenGoldenRules.com:

```
<title>Internet Marketing Consultant Online
Advertising Web Marketing and
Consulting</title>
```

The description tag should be 25 to 35 words that provide a brief summary of what the page is about (using keyword phrases) and a call to action.

```
<meta name="description" content="Internet
Marketing, Internet marketing blog, Consultant,
Online Advertising Strategy, Marketing,
Advertising, Banner and Ad design, improve
conversion, Search engine optimization, Free
Presentation The Ten Golden Rules of Online
Marketing. Written by Jay Berkowitz, CEO Ten
Golden Rules.com" />
```

The keyword tag is not really critical for most search engines. It can include 12 keyword phrases, including the company name and Website. Do not repeat any single word more than four times.

```
<meta name="keywords" content="internet
marketing, online advertising, consulting,
advertising, consultant, email marketing,
website marketing, marketing online, internet
marketing blog, jay berkowitz named business
```

```
journal heavy hitter in advertising and pr, ten
golden rules named prweb strategic partner,
search engine optimization, search engine
marketing, internet promotion services, web
site optimization, search engine optimization,
marketing consultancy, marketing consultants,
pr firm, public relations, interactive, public
speaking"/>
```

You can typically view these meta tags for any Website. In your browser's task bar, click on View > Source (or you can right click with your mouse). Hint: Viewing the source code is a good way to figure out what keywords your competitors are optimizing.

Advanced SEO Tips

With each Internet marketing tip, you'll also get one or more bonus advanced SEO tips! How's *that* for the icing on the cake?

Advanced Tip #1

Optimize Images and Videos

With the growing popularity and indexing of images and videos, search results have become increasingly blended. For example, I Google "Paris," and look what came up in

the search results: four pictures of socialite Paris Hilton
and two of the Eiffel Tower.

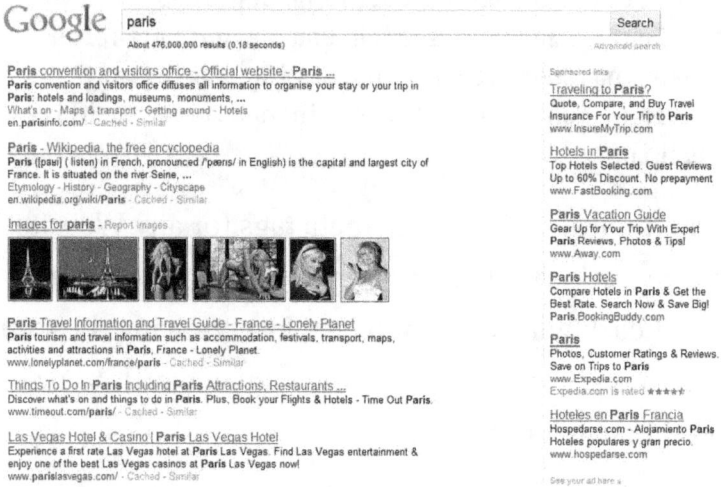

With "blended" search, results, it's now beneficial to optimize videos and
images. This search for "Paris" shows images of socialite Paris Hilton.

The lesson here is that Google is no longer only showing
word results. These types of results are called "Blended
Search." That's why it's critically important to **use**
targeted keyword phrases in the name of all of the
images on your site, including your videos and images
included with press releases.

Advanced Tip #2

Reputation Management

Reputation management is becoming increasingly important in Internet marketing. Reputation management is the strategy of proactively ensuring that your brand is protected on that all-important first page of Google.

Below, you'll see a search for "Jay Berkowitz." Our Website appears at number one and my personal blog, JayBerkowitz.com, comes in at number two. Also ranking in the search are my LinkedIn and Facebook Profiles, my Amazon Author's page, a Wall Street Journal article, and a listing for one of my presentations. So – I'm protecting my brand. This is a great strategy for your brands, your CEO, and for yourself.

Search Google for "Jay Berkowitz" and you'll find sites of mine and social media listings. "Google" your own name to check your online reputation.

#2:

Unique Value Proposition – UVP: Create a Free Offer on Your Site to Generate Leads

Everyone likes freebies, and giving something away that people perceive to be of value to them is a great way to generate valuable leads and Website traffic. **A unique value proposition – or UVP – is something free that people are going to take advantage of when they come to your site**.

Some examples of common UVPs include:

- Download something (eBook, free brochure, white paper, etc.)
- Enter a contest to win a prize
- Sign up for an eNewsletter

- Use a free calculator

This very book was originally written to be our UVP at
TenGoldenRules.com.

In exchange for the freebie, you ask people for their name and email address, to build a permission-based database and generate leads for your business. By opting in to your offer, visitors give you permission to email them on a regular basis.

If people are interested in your offer, not only will they interact with your Website, but they might even link to it from their site, their blog, or Twitter. In other words, **a UVP can be another powerful and effective way to build links to your site *and* boost your search engine rankings.**

Advanced Tip

Stair-step Your Marketing

A related strategy is **marketing stair-stepping**, in which you offer something free, with no strings attached. That means you don't ask for anything in return – no name, no email address, nothing.

Huh? "Why on earth would you want to do *that*?" you ask.

According to marketing guru, David Meerman Scott, if people like what you have to offer – let's say it's a free eBook download – then they're going to come back and subscribe to your newsletter or blog. Maybe they'll become a fan on your Facebook page or follow you on Twitter. They'll also be much more likely to buy your product or service.

#3:

Measure the Cost to Acquire a Lead (or a Sale)

One of the first things you want to determine as an Internet marketer is how much it costs to generate a lead or a sale.

If you sell items on your Website using eCommerce, you can measure direct Cost Per Sale. For example, if you spend $1,000 to advertise your Website and you generate 100 sales, your CPA, or Cost Per Sale, is $10.

If you sell Business-to-Business, you often have a two-step sales cycle; first step you get a lead, second step you have a sales presentation. Most business-to-business Websites focus on generating leads for their sales force to follow up.

In this example, you're measuring Cost Per Lead (CPL). Often, the Internet industry uses a blended terminology for both categories, called CPA or Cost Per Acquisition.

	Website Advertising ($)	Website Visits	Website Leads	Cost Per Lead (CPL)	Sales Meetings	New Customers
January	$2,656	11,256	246	$10.80	32	8
February	$2,789	13,250	294	$9.49	41	11
March	$3,156	14,072	343	$9.20	51	14

Google Analytics, also free, will show you your cost of lead acquisition.

You can measure your traffic and visitor behavior with **Google Analytics, which** is a **FREE and INVALUABLE tool**. (http://www.google.com/analytics).

Google Analytics measures: how many people are coming to your Website; what keyword they searched to get there; what pages and links they click on; which page they exit from; what your bounce rate is (the percentage of people who get to your Website, but don't view a second page); and more!

You *must* have Analytics on your site. All you have to do is sign up and, since it's *free*, it's a no-brainer.

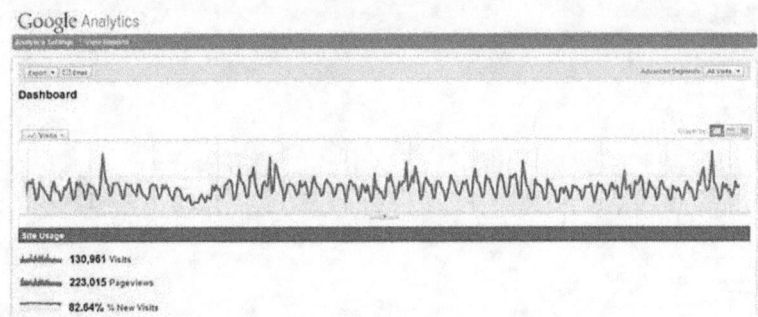

Google's free Google Analytics program is free and it's a must-have tool you need on your Website.

One of the fastest ways to measure Cost Per Lead is to test with **Google AdWords** Pay-Per-Click marketing (PPC), which is an ad, or "sponsored link," that appears on the right side of the page in Google search results.

Note that this is not 'free' – you pay every time someone clicks on your link. You can, however, spend as little as $25 and test the potential of this service to drive traffic to your site. The beauty of PPC is that you can advertise precisely to people searching for your product or service. You can also define exactly what your ad will say and where in the list of paid ads it will appear.

Test different keywords and ad copy, to measure clicks and, most important, conversion rates. With a simple code that you download from Google AdWords then place on your site, you can determine how much it costs to get a lead or a sale. In the example below, our cost per conversion is just $3.18.

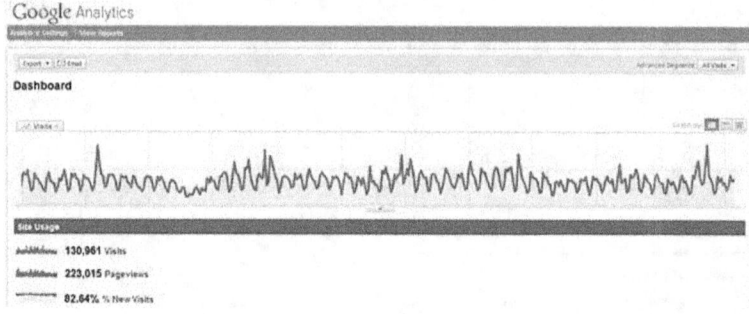

An example PPC test showing our cost per conversion is just $3.18.

Advanced Tip

Use Analytics to look at your sales funnel

An advanced measurement strategy is **funnel analysis**, which analyzes your sales funnel and conversions. Let's say you're selling t-shirts on your Website. Funnel analysis tells you how many people came to your Website, how many people went to each particular product page, how many people added an item to the shopping cart, and how many actually completed a purchase. In other words, it shows you how effective your Website is performing.

If you're testing different page designs, copy, content, navigation, or other factors, funnel analysis can be useful in determining which combination(s) are most effective at converting to leads or sales. It can even help highlight problem areas. For example: if, all of a sudden you experience a high percentage of people who bail on their shopping cart, this could indicate a problem with confidence in your secure credit card processing. Adding trust logos and security information might improve your conversion percentage.

#4:

Learn from the Competition

To learn from your competition, you can **spy on their Internet activity.** Yes, you read that right. Don't worry – it's all perfectly legal and most smart marketers do it.

Some tools I recommend include www.compete.com, www.SEOQuake.com, www.SEMRush.com, and www.spyfu.com. With Compete.com, you can view stats for unique visitors for free, but you'll have to pay for other metrics.

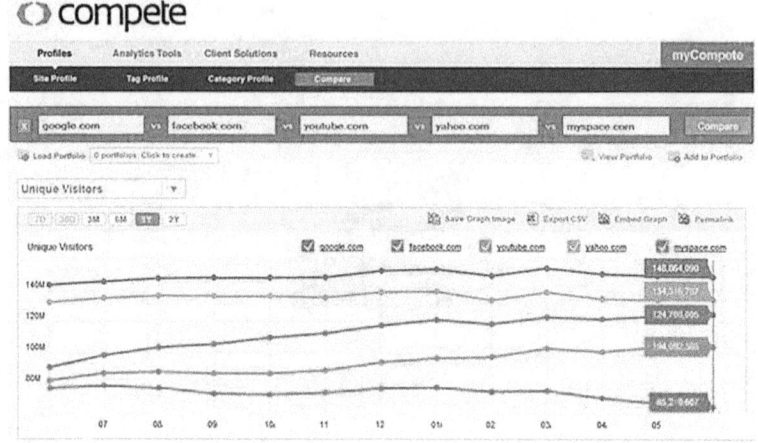

View competitors' unique visitor stats for free with Compete.com.

Key Website Measures: SEO Quake

SEO Quake.com is a handy toolbar that aggregates a number of key Website measures, including Google PageRank, Links *TO* your Website, Indexed Pages, Alexa ranking, Site Age, and many more, and shows them to you at a glance.

With a quick check of SEO Quake, we can see that TenGoldenRules.com is ranked as a 5/10 by Google's PageRank. This measures how important a Website is in Google's search engine, primarily evaluating the quantity, quality, and relevance of links from other sites. This is a tough scale. Five is very good.

The site has 126 pages indexed or 'read' by Google and it is ranked 162,899th in the world for traffic by Alexa.

The SEOQuake.com toolbar aggregates a number of key Website measures and makes it easy to see them at a glance.

Pay-Per-Click: SpyFu

With **SpyFu.com**, you can **see what your competitors are doing regarding pay-per-click advertising,** how much they spend, and which position in which their ads appear – all for free! Of course, SpyFu also offers paid subscriptions with additional metrics, such as ad copy and landing page links.

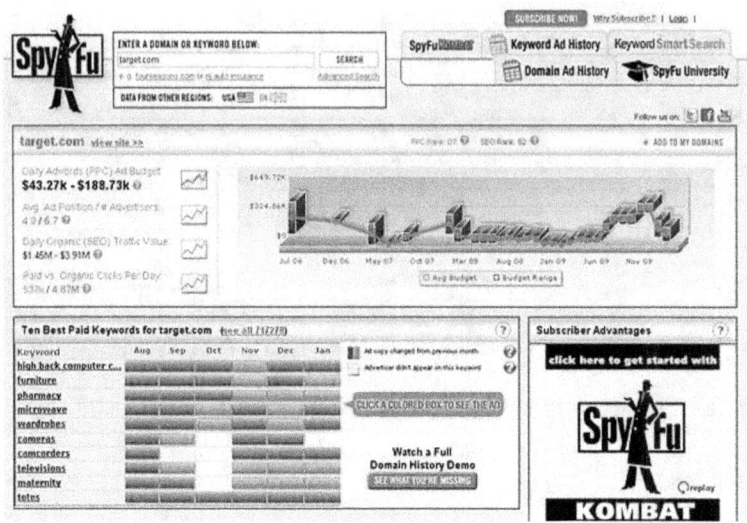

SpyFu.com shows you how much your competitors spend on pay-per-click advertising and which position in which their ads appear.

#5:

Use A:B Testing

The fastest way to improve your online performance is by testing two variables and determining a winner. You can test different offers, different prices, and different creative designs. This is **particularly effective for Landing Page Testing.**

With Google Content Experiments, available in Google Analytics, you can test a bunch of different variables, such as headlines, offers, copy, images, videos, buttons, calls to action, navigation, and more. Each variable is distinct. Content Experiments randomly serves different combinations of variables for a specified period of time (make sure it's long enough to collect statistically reliable information).

Google Content Experiments, available in Google Analytics, enables you to test a variety of distinct Website variables against one another.

For example, your test might show headline A, picture B, and button C (combination 1) to one visitor while another visitor sees headline C, picture A, and button B (combination 2). At the end of the test period, if combination 1 results in more conversions, you'd want to stick with that combination.

#6:

Send eNewsletters

Sending eNewsletters to your customers is a powerful addition to your Internet marketing program. Why?

- eNewsletters are a **UVP (Unique Value Proposition)**, a reason for people to sign up with you on your Website and to engage in a 'digital handshake' with you.

- When your customers sign up for your eNewsletter, they give **you permission to communicate with them.**

- eNewsletters are a perfect opportunity for you to stay top-of-mind with your customers and prospects. Just be sure to honor the trust relationship by sending them interesting, useful information that's relevant to their needs.

When you send an eNewsletter, there are two important elements to include: a **Forward to a Friend button** and functionality, plus a **call to action button or link**. What do you want your customers to do when they read the newsletter? Tell them!

Not only do you want to send these newsletters to your customers, but you also want to post the articles on your Website. **Adding new content to your site on a regular basis provides good "spider food" for the search engines** to read and rank. Just be sure to optimize your eNewsletter content for the search engines by including two to three keyword phrases, two or three times within 250 to 1,000 words of copy (see chapter 1).

Advanced Tip

Syndicate your Content

Take the same article you wrote for the eNewsletter and submit it to syndication sites like www.ezinearticles.com. It's free to submit articles. These syndication sites then make your articles available free of charge to other Websites. **Just be sure to post the article to your Website**

first, because you want Google to recognize your site as the origin of the content.

Why would someone else want to post *your* article on *their* Website? To add search engine content. These syndication sites are also a good source of content for your site, if you lack the time to write yourself or the money to pay someone else to write for you.

The best benefit of this approach? When people post your article, they must include your bio and **it creates a link to your site!**

#7:

Create a Virtual Sales Force

Affiliate marketing is a great way to increase traffic to your Website and generate leads for your business.

Let's say you sell scrapbooking supplies. You might want to create an affiliate relationship with wedding and event planners, scrapbooking Websites, online arts and crafts stores, scrapbook blogs, etc. Your "affiliates" will place banner ads or text links on their Websites or in their emails. Whenever someone clicks on those links to your site, you pay the affiliate a commission for every lead or sale they deliver to you.

To help you create your virtual sales force or become an affiliate yourself, you can try the following networks: www.shareasale.com, www.linkshare.com, www.cj.com, www.google.com/affiliatenetwork, or a multitude of other affiliate marketing sites.

Whether you're a merchant or want to become an affiliate, sites like these can connect you to quality partners.

#8:

Engage in Social Media

Social media sites present an excellent opportunity to drive free traffic (and revenue) for your brand. They can help you generate leads and build a community of customers, as well as connect to vendors and other businesses in your industry. There are a number of social media sites and tools you should take advantage of, including:

- Facebook
- YouTube
- Twitter
- LinkedIn
- Blogs
- Podcasts

Facebook

Facebook has two primary types of pages – personal profiles and business "Fan Pages." Facebook Fan Pages serve two major roles, among others:

1. First and foremost, you can expand your market and expose your business to new customers who otherwise may not have found you.
2. You can offer something valuable in return for those who click your 'Like' button, to become a fan of your page.

Targeted Facebook Ads

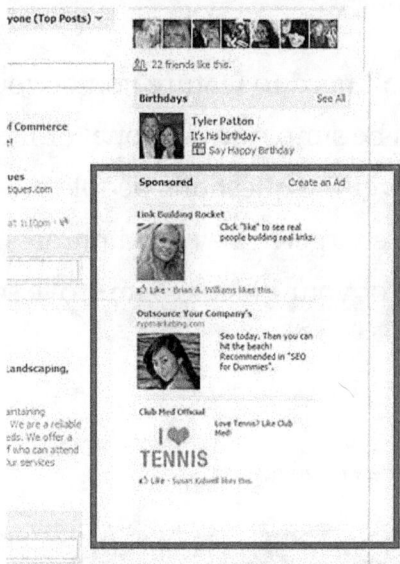

Facebook Advertising is one of the most exciting new opportunities for marketing on the Internet! You can target prospects based on their "Likes." The ads on this image would only show up for me ... I work in Internet marketing, I "Like" many Internet marketing Facebook Pages, and I am a big tennis fan and player.

Please note that Facebook Advertising is a paid service, it is not 'Free'.

YouTube

YouTube offers an amazing opportunity. The site is the #2 search engine (after Google) and the #3 most-visited site. You can post instructional videos for your product, or presentations that promote your services or establish you

as an expert in your field and post them on your own
YouTube Channel.

Your videos don't need to feature you or your CEO on-
screen; they can be simple educational or informational
videos that answer the questions people ask most about
your market. Use targeted keyword phrases in the name
and description of your videos to improve searchability of
your videos.

*With over 40 Million free YouTube views, tennis Website
FuzzyYellowBalls.com teaches tennis on the Internet! Each video invites
users to come to their Website and subscribe, to get more free instruction.
They have built a great business selling tennis courses to their list of
Website subscribers.*

Twitter

Twitter allows you to send 'Tweets' – messages of 140 characters or less – to your followers. You get instant updates from the people you are following and vice-versa. Twitter can be especially useful and timely for businesses. You can:

- Post daily updates on special offers
- Share real-time information about special events
- Communicate breaking news

A multi-million dollar Twitter success story is an online store called Woot.com. They only offer one product a day for sale and, each day, the item changes. They send out a Tweet announcing the product of the day and, almost every day, they sell out of that product.

LinkedIn

LinkedIn is the social network for professionals. By creating a profile for both you and your business, you can:

- Connect with others in your industry who are willing to share ideas and best practices

- Discover new business opportunities or business partners

- Find and be introduced to potential clients, vendors and industry experts

One great strategy for LinkedIn is to answer Questions in the LinkedIn Answers section of the site. Helping people is a great way to build relationships!

WORDPRESS.COM **Blogs**

A Blog is the simplest form of a Website that anyone can maintain—even with no technical skills. You can set up a blog in about fifteen minutes at WordPress.com. Blogs are a great tool for communicating with your customers and adding fresh content to your site on a regular basis.

Another way to use social media to generate revenue is to use Google AdSense within your blog. Whenever you see "Ads by Google" on a Web page, these are contextual ads triggered by words in the copy on the page. The page/blog owner is partnering with Google to generate revenue.

 **Podcasts**

I love podcasts! Podcasts are on-demand Internet radio shows that allow you to listen whenever and wherever you want. They are insightful, timely and most often free. By tuning in to the podcasts of the Internet marketing experts I follow, I can learn cutting-edge information while I'm stuck in traffic, on a treadmill at the gym, or walking my dog.

Over 20% of people listen to podcasts and, with new smart phones and iPhones sold every day, this market is expanding. The best news: a search for your industry in iTunes (the free podcast store) will likely find only 10-20 podcasts. What a great opportunity to stand out!

#9:

Create Web-Optimized Press Releases

The way people get their news has changed. Newspapers are struggling because so many people turn to the Internet these days to get their news. Not only are we as consumers going online to catch up on the daily news, but nearly all journalists use the Internet to research their stories. That's why online press releases can lead to offline public relations as well.

Additional **benefits of distributing online press releases** include:

- Fresh new content on your Website
- Increased traffic to your site
- External links to your site from sources that pick up your release and link to you

When you write a press release for your business, you want to treat it like any other content on your site:

(1) **Optimize it for the search engines.** You should know the drill by now: select two to three target keyword phrases and add them two to three times throughout your copy, plus your headline, sub-head, and meta tags.

(2) **Add it to your Website first,** so the search engines recognize you as the original source of the content.

The last step is to **use a good online press release service to distribute your story to the news wires**. There are plenty of them out there, and some offer basic services for free. A few that I have used include:

- www.PRWeb.com
- www.PRNewswire.com
- www.Businesswire.com

Some services have a broader reach than others. Your best bet is to experiment with a few and see which one(s) are most effective for you.

#10:

Build Your Personal Brand

Competition for jobs and business is fierce, but even more so in a down economy. Whether you work for a Fortune 500 company or you own a small business, it's vitally important to **establish yourself as an expert in your field**. You must **differentiate yourself and your company** to build your personal brand and stand out as an expert. Here are ten steps to help you do so:

1. **Be your own brand manager.** What have you done to position and improve your brand?

2. **Determine your USP. (Unique Selling Proposition)** What makes you distinctive and unique?

3. **Follow your passion.** If you do what you love, your enthusiasm will show and your personal brand and business will reap the rewards.

4. **Listen.** Get a feel for the environment and your customers' needs and concerns.

5. **Embrace your inner author and create unique content.** Write a blog or a free eBook. Submit articles to industry publications. Build great content on social media networks.

   I constantly create and publish a broad variety of information in all possible formats to build my brand and drive traffic to TenGoldenRules.com.

6. **Build your network.** Make quality connections both online and offline.

7. **Volunteer to shine.** Get involved with something you enjoy – whether it's an industry or work-related organization, a hobby-related group, or a charity. Do something you're already good at or something you want to learn more about to boost your skills and your brand.

8. **Innovate to lead. Test new technologies.** Stay on the leading edge of what's hot in your field of business.

9. **Entrepreneur.** Set up shop for yourself and be active online, whether you create a blog, become an affiliate marketer, regularly update your LinkedIn profile and Facebook fan page, etc.

10. **Speak up.** Take advantage of public speaking opportunities. My final advanced strategy: Read

Presentation Zen by Garr Reynolds. He's an excellent public speaking coach and offers a lot of simple but highly effective ideas for presentation design and delivery.

Wrap-up:

10 Free Strategies for Marketing on the Internet

1. Free Search Engine Optimization (SEO)

2. Create a free UVP (Unique Value Proposition)

3. Measure the Cost Per Lead

4. Learn from the Competition

5. A:B Testing

6. Create an eNewsletter

7. Create a Virtual Sales Force

8. Engage in Social Media

9. Create Web-Optimized Press Releases

10. Build your Personal Brand

Resources

Thanks for reading along. Mastering these 10 Tips for Marketing on the Internet will help you build the traffic and revenue you want without breaking the bank. For additional resources and the latest Internet marketing news, check out TenGoldenRules.com online.

Also:

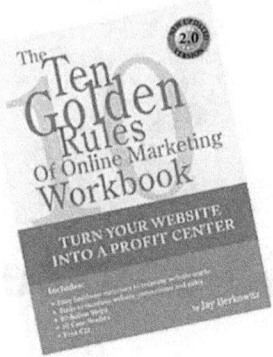

The Ten Golden Rules of Online Marketing
http://www.TenGoldenRules.com/order-book

"We saw Jay speak at eBay Live and purchased the book after the presentation. Since then, our sales have gone from barely ten thousand dollars per month to several hundred thousand per month."

—Bill Bayse, President, www.ShopFactoryDirect.com

"Your book, The Ten Golden Rules of Online Marketing, *is very informative, easy to read, understand, and implement. Great job!"*

—Dewayne Swinford Owner/Designer,
www.SwinfordTimePieces.com

"Excellent! I found this book very useful. A great read for an affiliate or an Internet marketer."

—Shawn Collins, Author, *Successful Affiliate Marketing for Merchants*, Co-Founder Affiliate Summit

For additional help and resources:

Web:
www.TenGoldenRules.com

Podcast:
http://podcast.tengoldenrules.com

Blog:
http://tengoldenrulesblog.blogspot.com

Twitter:
http://twitter.com/jayberkowitz (@JayBerkowitz)

YouTube:
http://www.youtube.com/tengoldenrules

Facebook:
http://www.facebook.com/tengoldenrules

LinkedIn:
http://www.linkedin.com/in/jayberkowitz

Books: *The Ten Golden Rules of Online Marketing Workbook*
http://www.TenGoldenRules.com/order-book

Email:
jay@tengoldenrules.com

www.ingramcontent.com/pod-product-compliance
Lightning Source LLC
Chambersburg PA
CBHW071815170526
45167CB00003B/1320